Still Looking for Neuzil

poems by

Michael Fredson

Finishing Line Press
Georgetown, Kentucky

Still Looking for Neuzil

1978-2018

ACKNOWLEDGMENTS

"Neuz Welcomes Me Home" was originally published as "My Vietnam
Buddy," which won honorable mention in Winning Writers War Poetry
Contest

"Neuz Welcomes Me Home," "Neuz Learns I Like The Doors," "Neuz
Phones His Old Buddies," "Neuz Offers Advice on Ghosts," "Neuzil and I
Visit Seattle," "Neuz Likes Some Parts of War," and "Neuzil Dreams for Me"
appeared in *Locuspoint*.

"A Ball, a Bat, and a Beer" appeared in *Pass in Review*.

"Ten Years After" and "Likeness" appeared in *Totem Tidings*.

"Freedom Bird" appeared as "Wind Song" in *Stone Country.*

"Killing the Beast" appeared as section 4 in "Walking Back" in *Writer's
Forum 5: New American Literature of the West.* Edited by Alexander
Blackburn (University of Colorado at Colorado Springs, 1978).

Publisher: Leah Huete de Maines
Editor: Christen Kincaid
Cover Art: Michael Fredson
Author Photo: Mya Lynn Keyzers
Cover Design: Elizabeth Maines McCleavy

Order online: www.finishinglinepress.com
        also available on amazon.com

Author inquiries and mail orders:
Finishing Line Press
P. O. Box 1626
Georgetown, Kentucky 40324
U. S. A.

Table of Contents

For
my dad, Paul Kenneth Fredson,

&

my mother, Alice Margaret Greenwalt Fredson (1920–1989),
who also learned to survive,

&

for all veterans
and your lifetime service of veteranship

"The war just keeps winning."

Paul Fussell,
The Great War and
Modern Memory

Anger & Self Delusion

NOT YOU (1)

In 1968 I am the one who low-crawled through November
      rains during Fort Lewis basic training.
I am the one who watched Christmas carols broadcast from
      a helicopter working the wire while the bunker line freefired
      tracer rounds that arced red then landed who-gives-a-shit-where.
I am the one who saw a medevac on the tarmac loaded with
      medics and wounded explode into a fireball that burned the
      bodies cinder black as they ran.
I am the one who spent nights in the underground bunker in water up to
      my knees,
And who had to low-crawl through the mud to get there and was grateful
      to do it.
I am the one who drove through a mortar ambush on QL 22
And refused to believe it happened.
I am the one who watched my buddy's hootch flattened by incoming;
My hootch was missed by a good twenty feet.
I am the one who shared the latrine with "gook" prisoners—the Marines
      called them "dinks"—
And who watched his base commander fly out every day before dusk.

ON THE OCCASION OF MY FIRST INCOMING

July 1969

I was born in Vietnam when Spec 4 Keller yelped "incoming"
And scared me out of my last stupid stateside sleep.
Boots unlaced, helmet web bouncing against my head,
Flak jacket hanging like a broken wing around one arm,
Canvas bandolier of ammo clips slapping on my shoulder,
I rushed into that VC night and down into the bunker
Like some clown costumed in a soldier's outfit.

Above, in my new world, mortar rounds
Searched me out and the earth moved
Like a belly trying to expel me.
In his underwear, Keller looked at me.
"This ain't Long Binh," he said, but nobody laughed
As the earth moved, searching us out.

A BALL, A BAT, AND A BEER

1

His hair curls like the crest
Of his aviator's cap, still boyish
Though thinning, and finally out of color
After these ninety years.
His 1938 Legion team won the state championship
With Dad in right field, trained to hit
By playing pepper with Uncle Spike.
Afterward, Dad brought beer from the bowling alley,
Bucket greased to keep the foam down,
Another good coaching tip.
When war came, Dad followed his big brother
Into the killing skies and came back
Twice from the dead, once over Yugoslavia,
When he gave his sidearm to his rescuers
Commenting *I could throw it more accurately than I could shoot it,*
And once after his plane was sabotaged on an Italian airfield.
His personal locker was ransacked
Because the orderly thought he was dead.
Black smoke smudged the sky and my dad's face
Until it could never be cleaned,
Even with the soap
Of two Distinguished Flying medals.

2

For years he fled that war
From bottle to bottle, drinking with his lost crewmen,
Their ghost hands still reaching from the burning cockpit
As he tried to return to Uncle Spike
And that game of pepper
Where there is a ball, a bat, and a beer
And nothing for your body to forget.
But Uncle Spike died during the war
From alcoholism, as old soldiers sometimes do.

Now each day, Dad, you hover on the couch
Like some memory that doesn't want to be recalled.

Surgeries fused your back rigid as a fuselage.
To relieve the pain of the plane crashes
You dose yourself daily with scotch, water, and buckets of beer.

LIKENESS

Braided into a Civil War uniform, your hair kinked
As mine, uncle to my grandfather,
I don't even know your name. Each day I glance at you,
Looking for me, and recognize the only story
I know. You marched toward Gettysburg and a bullet passed
Through the skulls of your flanking companions.
Your death was not needed, and you marched
Into this painting, too poor or unlucky
For the absence of your life to be photographed
In a Brady negative, though your eyes remain dark, skulled holes
Like any survivor.

LOOKING FOR NEUZIL

1 *The Rational*
Far in the mountains, confusing my left and right hands,
I bury my deepest secrets.
When I lower my eyes, search for my feet
And below my feet, clouds tumble about my ankles.
I am here; nowhere I can say: see, to the left, which is west,
The storm of water I love best, and in the air the smell of rain.

2 *The Unrational*
I look for someone to hide this secret from
To reveal to them, even as I lie to myself,
The darkness I sleep with is deeper,
More dear. Although I see no one,
I must believe someone hides in a direction I can't locate,
Watching me bury my *this,* helping me stay alive.

ANOTHER DAY (1)

Afternoon heat dries the day.
Crouching just under the horizon,
Hawks and cold ghosts.
All night they ride the wind,
Rattling front doors,
Singing to brothers in a howl.
The darkened stars are like mice
Crushed in their holes.
Young girls are dragged from back seats.
There is nothing else to do.

ANOTHER DAY (2)

I wait by my window
Listening every night.
If I close my eyes, my dreams
Stand watch over
The world of the agents of the dead.
In the morning, ghosts are left hanging
        in the branches.
My dreams have no hands.
At daylight, the ghosts
And I rise to live another day.
There is nothing else I can do.

NOT YOU (2)

I am the one who came home and learned he couldn't talk aloud about
       Vietnam,
Though every day it screamed in my head.
Who spends two hours a day in exercise and meditation to decide that
       suicide is not the answer today.
I am the one who loses his cart in Fred Meyer because of a panic attack.
I am the one who had a fainting spell driving in Nisqually Hill traffic
And who heard a doctor tell him it was a virus.
I am the one who wakes up at 3:00 a.m. because my body still remembers
       the incoming.
The one who wakes up with night sweats drenching the sheets.
The one who has wrecked his teeth by grinding them.
Who hears the chirping birds of tinnitus every second.
I am the one who doesn't talk to anyone he doesn't trust, and I don't talk
       to anyone.
I am the one who waits for the Agent Orange cancers.
I am the one who wakes up almost screaming.

Re-membering

*"America went to Vietnam a virgin,
and came home with the clap."*

Ron Cole,
folk philosopher

TEN YEARS AFTER

On her way home, a Vietnamese woman squats
To her knees' limits
And then squats farther. Among the dogs
And almond eyes a son emerges, his mouth
Clamped with refusals. His first storm
Of breath and his lungs want to refuse it
But can't. And so the woman licks
Off the old world he lived in, hard air of her body.

She offers the red moon
In the small sky of her breast
And he gums hard, his last hold on lunacy.
He is my son and his night cries
Swarm like peacocks around my dreams, his face
A moon always red and full and growing.

NEUZ WELCOMES ME HOME

July 1970

Neuzil, my Vietnam buddy, bused from Chicago,
Not thinking I wanted to leave him behind too.
He said his wife cheated, and that he had nowhere else to go,
While his finger picked at the air, as if picking a scab.

Soon he stopped talking until even my kids learned to ignore him.
At night, we watch Richard Widmark in *Halls of Montezuma,*
But we are never there.

When I say my children had dreams that I wouldn't save them,
He knows I am always awake, like a sentry. He is too.

When I have night sweats without dreams,
The kind you can't remember anything to be terrorized by,

But you are . . . he is so patient.
He brings a towel and checks on my sleeping wife.
Sergeant . . . young buck. He knows what will happen in the end.

NEUZ LEARNS I LIKE THE DOORS

December 1998

When I have fainting spells, he closes the door,
Helps me to my feet to face my wife and kids.
When they enter, he stands in my clothes
Because he knows shame has no disguise.

When they leave, he sits with me on the floor.
When I stare at the night
For tracers to knit the sky back together,
He looks for them too.

I tell him I like The Doors' "Five to One":
"You got the guns
But we got the numbers."

He so wants to be like me.
It is the only song he plays
Until it is the only song I want to hear.

NEUZ PHONES HIS OLD BUDDIES

December 1999

He began to wear my flannel shirts
Because they were baggy enough
For both of us to disappear into.
In my truck, we sat behind the windshield and
        the disguise it offered.

When he wore my Mariners hat, brim cupped
To the shape of my hand, a woman spoke to him
In some language he could almost understand.

He, too, knew alienation was a medal
That can't be shared with anyone.
When he phoned his old buddies,
They hung up.

I wanted to leave him behind, too,
But I became more like him each day.

NEUZ OFFERS ADVICE ON GHOSTS

February 2004

My hair turned from blond to dark,
As if it was my own. I spoke less
Of a vial of French amphetamine
And the monkey who gnawed its left finger off
Because Neuzil remembered too.

Soon my wife and kids no longer understood what we said.
Neuz and I began to carry dictionaries but didn't use them.
We spoke only to each other.

I don't like to listen
When he tells me how much easier it can be.

He says if I just listen to him
No longer would I feel the lost fingers of ghosts,
Almost hanging onto me,
Almost letting me go.

NEUZIL AND I VISIT SEATTLE

August 1970

Once I knew your face
Better than mine, its olive skin
The tinge of opium visions.
For 25 years I've never said your name;
I have no photos, only your laugh
Crackling like the love beads on stateside hippies.

Back in the World
With your beads and my field jacket,
A city cop demanded I remove the military insignia,
My only identity:
Incom-dodging, opium-smoking, clap-infected.

There was no World. No peace, love, and joy,
Only a patrolman pulling us over
For dropping a hitchhiker at the wrong exit.

NEUZIL AND I WATCH 2001: A SPACE ODYSSEY

April 1970

When I want to be alone I go
To where a thousand rounds explode, each night
A year's worth, for terror needs no memory
And dreams are no defense,
                              but there you are again,
Boonie hat, love beads, and a bracelet,
Huddled in the hootch watching *2001: A Space Odyssey,*
While outside, blind-eyed mortars searched
For the fear in all of us.

We'd lost our will to panic, as if we'd suddenly become old men
Whose lives had run out of hours.
We listen to the film
Click through the projector.
A mirage folds across the bare studs, boards, and wet canvas.

NEUZ LIKES SOME PARTS OF WAR

Neuz never visited Saigon, never wanted
Behind the bar girls and bar curtains:
Even if he missed the small canary
Birthing on stage from the pussy of some prostitute,
A mama-san who shoved military scrip up her butt like it was a purse.
Or the snake that wormed out and hung, midair, from the next,
Or the exotic dancer who wiggled a coke bottle
Up her ass. She would shake, uncap, and spray the audience,
Then remove the bottle.

He wasn't yet bored with the sweet obscenity of war.
At the security gate, the MPs would search the women with gloved fingers.
But not their assholes, as if in war there was at least one place too sacred,
even with gloves on.

NEUZ NEVER LEARNED TO JUGGLE

On July 1969, the same day astronauts landed
On the moon, I landed on the dark side of the earth
With three tennis balls to learn to juggle.

In my hootch, the gook ants
Nested in my water canteen
Like corpses, planting punji sticks
And tunneling down my throat.

With my squeeze bottle filled with gasoline
I squirted fire like napalm, incinerating ants
Jitterbugging down the drainage ditch.

Neuz, I never learned to juggle
—That everybody leaves
—That the dead remain with us
—That they are always out to get us
And that we become like them.

WHATEVER COMES FIRST

Soo, I waited for your lemongrass and buffalo dung
Fragrance on your *ao dai,* how you smuggled up
From Saigon by pedicab to love me you said,
As if saying anything makes it true.

It did for me at whatever price I wanted to pay.
Then you squatted over a water basin
And shoved that money up your ass

While the sun still burned a hole in the sky
For the incoming to fall through.
Outside, deuce-and-a-halfs churned up dust
That smelled like diesel as they hauled back to Long Binh.

When you left,
Again I took up waiting
For you, the convoy, the incoming, whichever comes next.

HOW I BECAME THE LUCKY GUY

I took incoming at the chow shack,
Free-flowing the QL 22 convoy route,
Leaning on the hood of a five-ton diesel truck,
Under a jeep repairing a universal joint again,
Joyriding the bunker line with the headlights off
(I bounced into the muddy ditch, oddly a fond memory).

At the 228th mess hall gagging on CS gas
Popped by our own bunker line,
On the floor goofy through the table legs,
Still spooning a mess hall tray of powdered eggs.

But I never took incoming while killing ants
Or smoking *camsa*, "the little treat."

BECAUSE IT SMELLED LIKE HOME

I returned to the World with a vial of perfume
Mixed with opium and the fetid water
Buffalo shit in.

Neuz, remember how Vietnam smelled like opium,
Water buffalo, unleaded gas, and the artillery smoke
That clung to our uniforms
Until we all smelled like home.

Opium turned our eyes yellow as urine
And the unleaded gas sank into our lungs.

ON SPEAKING TO STONES

I last spoke with stones during an ungodly storm
Of mortars that bounced a deuce-and-a-half
On back tires like a bronco
Bolting into a garden of white tracers.

Eye to eye, I asked the stone if I could I crawl beneath it,
But the stone never replied,
Prone, too, before the absolute authority of incoming.

Later I choppered over bomb craters filled with water
Reflecting that flat, blank look the eyes of survivors have.

But I don't remember rising from the mud and the incoming
To talk to each other, to practice being human again,
As if somehow that stone taught me
That any stone you chose to lie with
Will never answer.

Re-Cognition

"*For nothing is resolved, no conflict is settled, no remembering has become mere memory. What happened, happened. But that it happened cannot be so easily accepted. I rebel: against my past, against history, and against a present that places the incomprehensible in the cold storage of history.*"

Jean Améry,
At the Mind's Limit

NEUZIL HIDES IN MY BOONIE HAT

Some days when I look for you,
You are not there. When I call
I can't find you, it is because I want to be
Lost too, a war relic
That has become invisible because no one
Looks for it.

Years ago, I hid my boonie hat
In the closet from you,
Its brim bent down, its olive drab fabric
Thinned by years of neglect.
Today I look for you in old Super 8 movies,
Boonie hat shadowing my head,
My whole body vanishing in its shadow
As if I was never there.

NEUZ DREAMS FOR ME

Because I cannot dream, he kindly dreams
For me. He tells the dreams to me
As if they were his own
Until he believes they are.

When I accuse him of stealing my life
He tells me the dreams are only a Whirl-A-Gig
At the carnival.

The dead just reach through the glass
To pick up the toys. In the Hall of Mirrors
No one can see their reflections.

You will not be able to see them
Only for so long, Neuz says.
Soon you will look into an empty mirror.
You'll hear them calling *Save me*
In a voice that is your own.

BECAUSE I RARELY DREAM

Because I rarely dream, he dreams for me.
A man in a red hooded sweatshirt was stalking
Me again, he said,
As if he'd seen it before. I didn't want him
To finish, but he has to tell me.
He says the man is no danger,
I only feel chased
Because I flee every time
I see someone approach.
You know I'm your buddy, he says,
I only want to help you
Reach the pain you most try to mask.

NEUZIL IDENTIFIES FOUND PENNIES

Neuzil says the hooded shadow
With coins on his eyes
Has always been looking for you
Where trees are bleached
And where no thing lives.
Neuz says the hooded shadow lays on the ground
And looks for me like an underworld spy.

When I find pennies on the parking lots,
It is his one eye
Following me as I pick it up.
It stares at me
As if it were finally home.

NEUZ LIKES TO WEAR CAMO

In a voice I still listen to, Neuz tells me
Incoming can only harm bodies caged in fatigues.
Unblouse your trousers, discard your underwear, he says,
The hootch maids will steal them anyway.

Become like a ghost warrior. Wear the hide
Of the animal dead
Invisible in that world
Where the dead have their place
And the living need disguises.

The dead recognize me
As one of their own, he says.
Wear camouflage trousers,
He says, they can't see you,
They think you are me.

NEUZIL DISGUISED AS UNINVITED GUEST

Some days you just don't want to remember
The old days, but I need you
Because you are my best friend.
You sleep on the sofa,
Clean out the refrigerator,
Watch late-night TV
Like any uninvited guest.
You remember every day
I want to forget.

With you, I am invisible.
Without you, I am invisible.

Here we live forever, Neuz says,
We can talk to each other and no one knows,
And if we never speak,
That, too, will be enough.

NOT HERE

Neuz, if I deny you long enough
I will be emptied
Of the only thing
That is my own
And that I can continue to hide
And to hide from.

You are my only companion
I can never abandon.
You have taught me
How not to be here
Where I don't belong anyway.

I HEAR NEUZIL ON THE RADIO

Neuz, you are like some scratchy radio I can't turn off,
Translating that language of the lost,
The dead, the potheads, and the whores,
Listening for the incoming we never hear soon enough?
Every night I try to leave you
But you stay, a frequency in my head, broadcasting memories,
Keeping me safe from ever feeling safe again.

NEUZIL WANTS TO BE A TOUR GUIDE

Neuz says you can't go home anymore,
Your daughter lives in the house you built.
Return with me, he says, to Tay Ninh,
We'll dodge incoming and scuff through dust.

Neuz, I say, I've been back; there's no Vietnam anymore,
No water buffalo. Tractors plow the rice paddies.
Now the country smells like another home.
Tay Ninh Base Camp is off-limits;
Now the Cambodian sanctuaries hide
Sun bears, bile extracted to sell to the Chinese.

Wherever you go, Neuz says, is not home.
Wherever you don't go, he says, you don't belong either.

BASE CAMP WARRIOR

In Tay Ninh, when a mortar dropped on an evac helicopter,
McClain and I drove our jeep from the target zone
And never spoke of it again
As if it never happened and we were never there.

NEUZIL APPEARS AFTER ALL THESE YEARS

After all this time, there you are again,
Cursing in your voice only I can hear.
The color of damnation envelops you
And you seal me off from ever seeing you again.

Mike, when you phoned, I hung up.
The air you breathe on me
Coats my skin and seals my mouth like dust.

MANNEQUINS CAN'T TALK

for Terri

Neuz, when I haven't seen you lately
I visit displays of mannequins at the mall
Because we have so much in common.

The mannequins dress in other people's clothing
To masquerade as a human
No one can quite recognize.

In a language they don't know
I understand,
They yell *"run"* when I approach,

but they can't. If they move, they will reveal,
Even as they hide from themselves,
That they are still encased by the shame of surviving.

So when the mannequins wave their hands,
They are really motioning *"go away."*

Resignation

"You have need of endurance..."

Hebrews 10:36

DEAR TAY NINH DUST

The convoy wheels trailers into the yard,
Hauling America's best:
Pallets of ammunition and cases of Coca-Cola.
Their tires raise a fog of dust
That suffocates the creases of my face
Like a mask,
As if it is makeup
Applied by the mortician on a corpse
Not yet dead.

Back in the World
Women shelter their children
When I appear,
As if the mortician missed a spot
And death shows through its mask.

NEUZ MEETS AN APOSTLE

The old lifer's face emerges from the cumulous
That smells like Winstons, the brand grunts smoke,
Not the menthol-filtered Salems
The papa-sans liked.

Sometimes it takes decades, the lifer said,
His voice burned by ten thousand evenings of whiskey,
But the Beast will come

Without warning. My first time, the lifer said,
I suddenly blacked out, weakened
By the Beast, who like some biological parasite
No longer needing my carcass,
Left it discarded on the bathroom floor
As if it was still taking incoming.

The booze really feeds the Beast, the lifer said,
Until you can't think
You can even live without it.

KILLING THE BEAST

I said in mine heart concerning the estate of men,
that they might see that they themselves are beasts.

Ecclesiastes 3:18

The night the wind blacked out
The hospital,
My birth was Cesarean.
Mother died, refusing
The rosary of priests.
Grandfather claimed me as son.

For years I slept in my grandfather's house,
Prowled the attic,
Listening to the moon
Tap across shingles.

After men trapped you in sleep,
Gutted you,
Intestines and liver left behind,
Blood caught in a pail,
They hauled you out,
Again human.
To keep me from you,
Father buried his vial
In the attic.
When he showed the vial,
The blood
Crawled up the tube.
When I held that blood,
My hand itching,
That terrible howl
Opened in my throat.

ANXIETY HAS EIGHT LEGS AND ANTENNAS

In tight black pajamas
And waving their swords over their heads,
The ant monks
Nibble on the edges of my dreams,
Communion wafers offering something like
            eternal life

As they chant
Fuck you, fuck you, fuck you,
Fuck you, fuck you, fuck you.

Neuz lives in the land of ants.
All day I smash at them
Inside cabinets and above the bathtub.

That is the worst; they hide in the dark
Of my brain again. They are only there
Because you see them, Neuz says,
Not because they are real.

BACK IN THE WORLD

Neuz, when I came back to the World
I didn't know how to act
So I acted like you.

I dressed in your camos
Like a criminal uniform I still needed to wear.

Like that LRRP grunt at Ben Kao, silent
In the shadows of his hootch,
I lived in the dead sun,
But I wanted to come home
And no longer speak my pidgin gook.

Don't bother, Neuzil says, no one wants to talk to you
If you can't dress right
Or don't speak the language.

CONG THE SERVICE DOG

Neuz, remember Cong,
That mutt with matted black hair that liked to lap up beer?
You and me and Cong watched the special forces camp on
        top of Nui Bau Dinh Mountain
Light up with white tracers and bouncing red RPG rounds.

For years I fled from my own fear
Like any good soldier waiting for the war to pass,
While Cong cowered in the corner
And mocked my fear like a mute imitating his only memory.

By then other people couldn't see the dog
And thought me mad
When I barked to shoo the dog away.
Cong just stared back,
Poised to strike the only person who could see him.

NEUZIL IS HOME

I drive the same blue Chevy truck
So I never age
Sitting in the same seat, dialing the same radio stations.
I always drive the same route
Even if it doesn't take me where I'm going.

The Beast tracks my scent
Heavy from the night sweats,
A baptism font of wet sheets.

MAILING MY UNIFORM

Neuz, no one remembers
Your last days
Sheltered under convoy trailers
On Orange Sunshine.

I mailed home envelopes of rolled jays
To trade for the acid
To help you prepare
To be a stateside hippie, headband and all.

When Terry DEROSed from Tay Ninh's MP detachment
I mailed his speakers to his New York home
Stuffed with pot.

When my DEROS date approached
I mailed a C ration box
Of camo trousers and fatigue jackets
Packed with bags of *camsa*.

When the mail clerk
Filled out the mail tag, he confirmed
Without looking up,
"This is your uniform?"

NEUZIL IS SHORT

When you left base camp, I left too,
Though I was still 60 days short.
I shuffled the dusty camp roads
Each day to the PX to buy Sweet Tarts
As if already I was back in the world.

When a mortar dropped on an evac helicopter,
The fireball blackened their bodies
And their spirits *di-di-ed* that fireball fast; I hopped in the
        jeep and left too.

When a rocket smashed the end of my buddy's hootch,
I kept walking. I knew he was already gone and I was too.

When the gooks attacked the wire, I couldn't stop laughing
Because it wasn't really happening.

Back in the World, when my wife left me,
I could only laugh.

WHERE THE ANTS GO

The ants' antennae twitch like arm hair
As they crawl the ditches beneath my skin.

NEUZ LIKES FOURTH OF JULY

Overhead, fireworks burst into streams of fire.
The first burst of firecrackers pop off
And white tracers streak through my brain,

My heart converts to arrhythmia,
Like spare ammo,
Set to explode without warning.

NEUZIL IS LISTED AS DECEASED

for Mike

Years ago, you phoned, recalled our Thanksgiving
Patrolling in the MP jeep with Stumpy and Spec 5 Lamb,
Sharing a baguette, spaghetti without sauce,
And a vial of maxiton 4—French amphetamine.
Drinking in a combat zone, I know,
Is hazardous to your health.

When I phoned back just a decade later,
Your number had been disconnected.

GOING TO REHAB

Neuz, when I lost touch with you
I went to rehab,
Tired of listening to the dead
Tell me how easy it is.

Each morning, I drive the I-5 freeway,
Dodging Datsuns, steering through the blockade of
        double semis
That look like they could digest my little Honda
And spit it out the rear duals
Like Lenz, the New York junkie, did to the papa-san
        and his motorbike
On the way to Ben Keo.

At the VA, we talk about self-forgiveness,
And I start sobbing again for no good reason.

NEUZIL GOES HOME

Agent Orange discolors our blood
With toxins that glow in the dark of the dead:
Dave Waite, Bob Bryant, Ben Myers.

Now my toes are numb and cold and red
From peripheral nephropathy:
I can walk barefoot on hot desert pavement,
The first step toward eternity,
Where no one is ever dead
Because they already are.

FREEDOM BIRD

I come with the wind, bend fir boughs
Until they moan, rip twigs loose with my fingers.
I tear feathers from birds, lofting
The bodies by their wings into the cold grasp of space.
I burrow through the dark, each shovelful
Falling toward the sky, the tunnel filling behind me.

Rich with wandering, lost to the anchor of a home,
Each day I am farther from where I want to be. When I speak
Wind tears words from my ears. I have heard the silence so long
It is an echo.
              By moving I cease to move,
Feathers gather in the shoals about my arms and I rise,
Growing colder as the stars fall toward me.
Is this dying or birth? I have no maps, no charts,
I know only the currents of the wind, the drifts that never cease.

Pro-logue

I RIDE SHOTGUN

Hitching back to Tay Ninh from Long Binh,
The driver asked if I'd ever been in an ambush.
No, I told him but wasn't worried,
I'd been in-country seven months.
An ambush is a real trip, he said,
You duck your head and drive like hell.

When we went through Goa Dau Hau,
A crippled man on all fours
Scurried in front of us like a crab,
Crawling into an alley faster than I can run.

At the staging area, the convoy commander said
A satchel charge thrown on a JP-4 tanker
At Goa Dau Hau fell off before it exploded.

Don't mean nothin', I said.

NOTES

The book's epigraph is from Paul Fussell's *The Great War and Modern Memory* (New York: Oxford University Press, 1975). Fussell received a Bronze Star and a Purple Heart in World War II.

The epigraph at the beginning of Re-Cognition is from *At the Mind's Limit: Contemplation by a Survivor on Auschwitz and Its Realities* by Jean Améry (Bloomington: University of Indiana Press, 1980). It is the English translation of *Jenseits von Schuld und Suhne: Bewältigungsversuche eines Überwältigten,* originally published in 1966.

Améry was tortured and yet survived the German concentration camps of Auschwitz and Buchenwald. After the war, he changed his name from Hanns Mayer to Jean Améry (which means "bitter" in French). He committed suicide in 1978.

Whatever Comes First
A deuce-and-a-half is a 2½-ton truck.

How I Became the Lucky Guy
*Cams*a is GI pidgin for marijuana.

Back in the World
LRRP is Long Range Reconnaissance Patrol.

Cong the Service Dog
RPG is Rocket Propelled Grenade.

Mailing My Uniform
DEROS is Date Estimated Return Overseas.

Neuzil Is Short
Di-di means "to leave immediately."

Michael Fredson is a VA-rated totally disabled Vietnam veteran who served in 1969-70 in Tay Ninh. Fredson received his MFA from University of Arizona in 1978. He is the author of several local history books about his home in Washington state. He lives on Hood Canal and is the father of two children.

www.ingramcontent.com/pod-product-compliance
Lightning Source LLC
Chambersburg PA
CBHW021158090426
42740CB00008B/1149